A Guide for Using

Crash

in the Classroom

Based on the novel by Jerry Spinelli

This guide written collaboratively by

Kathleen B. Quinn, Ph.D.   **Bernadette Barone, M. Ed.**

Janine Kearns, M. Ed.   **Susan Stackhouse, M. Ed.**

Marie Zimmerman, M. Ed.

Teacher Created Materials

Teacher Created Materials, Inc.
6421 Industry Way
Westminster, CA 92683
www.teachercreated.com
©2004 Teacher Created Materials
Made in U.S.A.
ISBN 0-7439-3163-7

Edited by
Melissa Hart, M.F.A.

Illustrated by
Sue Fullam

Cover Art by
Kevin Barnes

Table of Contents

Introduction

A good book can touch our lives like a good friend. Within its pages are words and characters that can inspire us to achieve our highest ideals. We can turn to it for companionship, recreation, comfort, and guidance. It can also give us a cherished story to hold in our hearts forever. *Crash* can do all of these things, as well as help your students to understand the problem of bullying and to find ways to prevent it.

In Literature Units, great care has been taken to select books that are sure to become good friends!

Teachers who use this unit will find the following features to supplement their own valuable ideas:

- Sample Lesson Plans

- Pre-reading Activities

- A biographical sketch and picture of the author

- A Book Summary

- Vocabulary Lists and Suggested Vocabulary Activities

- Chapters grouped for study with each section including:
    —quizzes
    —hands-on projects
    —cooperative learning activities
    —cross-curricular connections
    —extensions into the reader's life
    —an emphasis on writing and critical thinking

- Post-reading Activities

- Book Report Ideas

- Culminating Activities

- Three Different Options for Unit Tests

- Bibliography Resources

- Answer Key

We are confident that this unit will be a valuable addition to your planning, and we hope that it will inspire your students to increase the circle of "friends" they have in books and among their classmates!

Sample Lesson Plan

The time it takes to complete the suggested lessons below will vary, depending on the type of activity, your students' abilities, and their interest levels.

Lesson 1

- Introduce and complete some or all of the pre-reading activities from "Before the Book" on page 5.
- Read about the author with your students on page 6.
- Review the vocabulary from Section 1 with your students, on page 8, and do vocabulary activities on page 9.

Lesson 2

- Read Chapters 1–8. As you read, place the vocabulary words in the context of the story and discuss their meanings. Discuss key ideas about the characters, setting, and plot. Help your students make personal connections during the discussions.
- Create life-size models of Crash and Penn on page 11.
- Have fun with football on page 12.
- Substitute synonyms in the context of the novel on page 13.
- Decide whether you would be Crash or Penn on page 14.
- Administer the quiz for Section 1 on page 10.
- Preview the vocabulary from Section 2 with your students, on page 8, and do vocabulary activities on page 9.

Lesson 3

- Read Chapters 9–18. As you read, place the vocabulary words in the context of the story and discuss their meanings. Discuss key ideas about the characters, setting, and plot. Help your students make personal connections during the discussions.
- Create a comic strip on page 16.
- Learn about recycling on page 17.
- Apply math skills to football on page 18.
- Learn to believe in yourself on page 19.
- Administer the quiz for Section 2 on page 15.
- Preview the vocabulary from Section 3 with your students, on page 8, and do vocabulary activities on page 9.

Lesson 4

- Read Chapters 19–30. As you read, place the vocabulary words in the context of the story and discuss their meanings. Discuss key ideas about the characters, setting, and plot. Help your students make personal connections during the discussions.
- Make a protest poster on page 21.
- Compare Pennsylvania and North Dakota on page 22.
- Learn about Quakers on page 23.
- Explore character motivation on page 24.

- Administer the quiz for Section 3 on page 20.
- Preview the vocabulary from Section 4 with your students, on page 8, and do vocabulary activities on page 9.

Lesson 5

- Read Chapters 31–43. As you read, place the vocabulary words in the context of the story and discuss their meanings. Discuss key ideas about the characters, setting, and plot. Help your students make personal connections during the discussions.
- Build a wildlife habitat on page 26.
- Make catfish cakes on page 27.
- Visualize a scene from the novel on page 28.
- Write about a meaningful person on page 29.
- Administer the quiz for Section 4 on page 25.
- Preview the vocabulary from Section 5 with your students, on page 8, and do vocabulary activities on page 9.

Lesson 6

- Read Chapters 44–49. As you read, place the vocabulary words in the context of the story and discuss their meanings. Discuss key ideas about the characters, setting, and plot. Help your students make personal connections during the discussions.
- Create a family portrait on page 31.
- Act out scenes from the novel on page 32.
- Compose a cinquain on page 33.
- Make a family stew bag on page 34.
- Administer the quiz for Section 5 on page 30.

Lesson 7

- Discuss any questions your students have about the novel on page 35.
- Assign book reports and research projects from pages 36 and 37.
- Do some or all of the culminating activities on pages 38–42.

Lesson 8

- Administer Unit Tests 1, 2, and/or 3 on pages 43–45.
- Discuss the test answers and possibilities.
- Discuss the students' enjoyment of the book and encourage them to compare and contrast it with books they have read.
- Provide a list of related reading for your students, on page 46.

Before the Book

Before you begin reading *Crash* with your students, complete one or more of the following pre-reading activities to stimulate their interest and enhance comprehension.

1. Discuss the topic of bullying. What is bullying? Who usually does it? How does it feel to be the victim of a bully? How does it feel to be a bully? Why might someone become a bully?

2. Show a clip from a movie, television show, or cartoon that depicts the theme of bullying. Discuss the events in the scene. Identify the victim, bully, and bystanders.

3. William Penn is a famous Quaker whom the students may be familiar with from Social Studies. The Quakers brought their religion to Pennsylvania when William Penn first acquired the land in Pennsylvania. Penn Webb, one of the main characters in the novel, is a Quaker. Have students research Quakers and their religious beliefs at the library.

4. Vegetarianism is widespread today; and students may know someone who is a vegetarian or they may be vegetarians themselves. One of the main characters in the novel is a vegetarian. Discuss the components of a vegetarian diet, and brainstorm reasons why people become vegetarians.

5. The Penn Relays are track-and-field events held every spring at the University of Pennsylvania in Philadelphia. Have students find out the history of the Penn Relays, where they are held, what events are held, who may participate, and how long they have been in existence. Invite a track coach to visit your class, and ask students to prepare a list of questions for the visitor.

6. Penn Webb takes a stand to protest an impending shopping mall. He and his friends protest the building of the new mall. Encourage students to brainstorm protests they are aware of either locally or nationally. Have them research famous protests that have changed our nation. You might wish to encourage them to write letters of protest themselves.

7. Penn Webb joins the cheerleading squad, and Crash makes fun of him. Poll the students to determine their opinion of boys joining the cheerleading squad. Have students create a survey sheet and poll peers outside of class for other opinions. Calculate the findings, share, and discuss the results. Ask students what might be responsible for public opinion regarding cheerleaders. You might also ask students to research college cheerleading squads and determine the ratio of males to females.

8. Scooter, Crash's grandfather, suffers a stroke that changes his life. Have students research what happens to a body when it suffers a stroke. What causes a stroke? What are the short- and long-term consequences of a stroke? Do specific warning signs indicate that someone may be experiencing a stroke? Ask students to share stories about people they know who have suffered from a stroke. Discuss appropriate ways in which students can help stroke victims.

About the Author

Jerry Spinelli

Jerry Spinelli was born on February 1, 1941, in Norristown, Pennsylvania. This is where he grew up. It is also the setting of many of his novels, including his Newbery Award Winner, *Maniac Magee*. (He also won the North Dakota, "Flicker Tale" Award for the novel in 1994.) *Crash* also takes place in Norristown.

As a child, Jerry loved baseball, football, basketball, and track. This appreciation for sports is reflected in his novels. He played on many teams throughout school and did especially well in grade school and middle school. In high school, he continued to play, but he admits that he was no longer "a star."

Jerry also enjoyed exploring his neighborhood's parks and alleys, whether on foot or on bicycle. He had many friends and would often explore with them or on his own. He had a fascination with discovering new places to go and new things to do, like looking for leeches in a pond or finding an unusual route home from school.

Like many children of his era, Jerry liked listening to the radio, going to see cowboy movies, and watching TV. He often played games based on the shows he watched. He never lacked an imagination.

Jerry attended the public schools of Norristown, where he was a good student. He liked to read comic books such as "Bugs Bunny" and comic strips, the "funnies" in the newspaper, and cereal boxes! As he got older, he enjoyed the sports section of the newspaper, as well.

Jerry began writing when he was sixteen. After his high school football team won an important game, his classmates ran through the streets cheering. Jerry found his own way of celebrating. He went home and wrote a poem about the victory, and the poem was published in the local paper. It was then that Jerry decided to become a writer instead of a major-league shortstop.

After graduating from high school, Jerry went to Gettysburg College and Johns Hopkins University. He got a job as a magazine writer and began writing novels on the side. He married a writer, Eileen, and had seven children. After writing four adult novels, he found his "niche"—writing children's books. His first published novel was *Space Station Seventh Grade*. He hasn't stopped writing since.

Jerry's childhood has had a definite influence on the characters in his novels, including *Crash*. He writes about feelings and events from his own childhood, and uses his own children for inspiration. For more on Jerry Spinelli's life, read his autobiography, *Knots in My Yo-Yo String*, and visit his Web site: *http://www.carr.lib.md.us/authco/spinelli-j.htm*

Crash

By Jerry Spinelli

(Random House, 1996)

Crash takes place in a Pennsylvanian suburb. The story centers around two main characters, John "Crash" Coogan and Penn Webb. Crash and Penn meet at the age of seven, when Penn moves into Crash's neighborhood. Crash takes an immediate dislike to the new kid on the block. He immediately rips off a button on Penn's shirt. He is confused by Penn's unwillingness to fight, and by his family. The Webbs do not eat meat. Even stranger, they don't have a television.

Mike DeLuca moves into the neighborhood when Crash and Penn are in middle school. Mike and Crash plan ways to tease and bully Penn. Crash and Mike have much in common, and both become star jocks on the football team. Much to their amusement, Penn becomes a cheerleader. Jane, an attractive new girl in school, impresses Crash with her mature demeanor. However, Jane prefers to spend time with Penn and Crash's sister, Abby—the three of them attempt to prevent the building of a new mall. Jane wants nothing to do with Crash.

Crash's parents are busy and preoccupied with their jobs. Then Crash's grandfather, Scooter, moves in with the Coogan family. Crash loves his grandfather and appreciates the man's sincere interest, time, attention, and affection. He's glad that someone in his family appreciates his incredible abilities on the football field.

Unexpectedly, Crash's grandfather suffers a stroke and is hospitalized. It is then that Crash begins to change his self-centered attitude. He tries to help his little sister and stops bullying Penn Webb. He witnesses a transformation within his family, as they rally around his sick grandfather. Because of Scooter's stroke, Crash begins to understand Penn and his love for his family, including his own grandfather who once ran in the Penn Relays.

Crash surprises himself at the end of the novel by making the ultimate sacrifice . . . for Penn Webb.

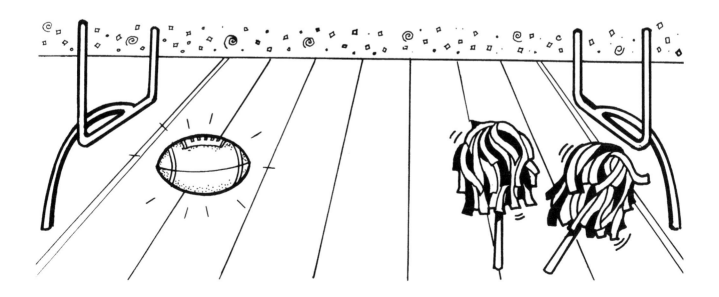

Vocabulary Lists

This page contains vocabulary words that correspond to each section of the book.

Section 1: Chapters 1–8

scrawny	misery
prairie	combination
bamboozled	infantry
Quaker	Amish
violence	pestering
glum	species
vegetarian	shuddered
consume	

Section 2: Chapters 9–18

loose cannon	sneered
defensive back	snooty
smirked	poacher
scowled	sputtered
proceed	lugged
tormented	paydirt
pries	waded
forfeit	

Section 3: Chapters 19–30

scrumptious	Achilles
fluorescent	pathetic
anaconda	obnoxious
Borneo	wallowing
forlorn	fumble
swoon	campaign
habitat	vermin
smirking	hoisted
rouge	rodent

Section 4: Chapters 31–43

stroke	blubbered
demon	sprinter
woozy	pneumonia
klutzy	thrift shop
legend	frantically
jabbered	demolish
clammy	plowing
bulged	

Section 5: Chapters 44–49

hurricane	baton
bonkers	gasp
groping	heave
tradition	pennants
automatically	regretted
possibilities	suspicious
nervous	

Vocabulary Activity Ideas

You can help your students learn the vocabulary words in *Crash* by providing them with the stimulating vocabulary activities below.

- Ask your students to work in groups to create an illustrated book of the vocabulary words and their meanings.

- Separate students into groups. Use the vocabulary words to create crossword puzzles and word searches. Groups can then trade puzzles with each other and complete them.

- Play "Guess the Definition." One student writes down the correct definition of the vocabulary word. The others write down false definitions, close enough to the original definition that their classmates might be fooled. Read all definitions, and then challenge students to guess the correct one. The students whose definitions mislead their classmates get a point for each student fooled.

- Use the word in five different sentences. Compare sentences and discuss.

- Write a short story using as many of the words as possible. Students may then read their stories in groups.

- Encourage your students to use each new vocabulary word in a conversation five times during one day. They can take notes on how and when the word was used, and then share their experience with the class.

- Play Vocabulary Charades. Each student or group of students gets a word to act out. Other students must guess the word.

- Play Vocabulary Pictures. Each student or group of students must draw a picture representing a word on the chalkboard or on paper. Other students must guess the word.

- Challenge students to a Vocabulary Bee. In groups or separately, students must spell the word correctly and give its proper definition.

- Talk about the different forms that a word may take. For instance, some words may function as nouns, as well as verbs. The word "shroud" is a good example of a word which can be both a noun and a verb. Some words which look alike may have completely different meanings; in *Crash*, "stroke" refers to a medical problem, but it can also function as a verb which means "to caress."

- Ask your students to make flash cards with the word printed on one side and the definition printed on the other. Ask your students to work with a younger class to help them learn the definitions of the new words, using the flash cards.

- Write the words with glue on stiff paper, and then cover the glue with glitter or sand. Alternatively, students may write the words with a squeeze bottle full of jam on bread to create an edible lesson!

Quiz Time

Answer the following questions about Chapters 1-8.

1. How does Crash get his nickname?

_____

_____

2. How do Crash and Penn Webb meet?

_____

_____

3. Who tells Penn Crash's real name? Why is Crash mad?

_____

_____

4. Why can't Penn have a water gun fight with Crash?

_____

_____

5. What surprises Crash about the race between him and Penn? Why?

_____

_____

6. What is Penn's family like?

_____

_____

7. Why can't Crash's father take him to the Phillies game?

_____

_____

8. How is Mike DeLuca different from Penn?

_____

_____

10

Paper Dolls

In the first section of the novel, you learn a great deal about Crash and Penn. They are very different characters, with particular hobbies and philosophies. Make life-sized models of Crash and Penn, using what you know about each character to bring your paper doll to life.

Materials

- index cards
- paper
- large sheets of butcher paper, at least 5" (1.5 m) long
- pencils
- yarn
- paper bags
- string, ribbon
- glue, stapler, staples, scissors
- markers, paints, crayons, and colored pencils
- buttons

Directions

1. Form groups of four students.

2. Review section one of *Crash*. Identify important characteristics which define either Crash or Penn. List your chosen character's traits on an index card.

3. Now, sketch the character and discuss how he should be pictured.

4. Make a list of items necessary to construct a model of your character.

5. Trace a life-sized model of either Crash or Penn on butcher paper. (You may want to use one person in your group as a model.) Cut out and dress your model. Add a face, hair, and other defining characteristics. For instance, Penn always wears a button on his shirt, and Crash wears sports attire.

6. Share your model with the class, explaining your character's physical and emotional traits.

Teacher Note: Models can be kept on display throughout the reading of this novel. You may encourage students to add or subtract items from these models as they read and gather more information about each character.

Fun with Football

Played by professionals and amateurs, American football is a wildly popular sport, attracting thousands of participants and millions of spectators annually. People all across the country watch the Super Bowl every January, and many junior high and high schools have amateur football teams.

The ancient Greeks used to play *harpaston*—a game similar to American football. In this game, there was no limit to the number of players. The object was to move a ball across a goal line by kicking, throwing, or running with it. Classical literature contains detailed accounts of the game, including descriptions of ferocious tackling.

American football developed in the United States in the 19th century as a combination of soccer and rugby. Interestingly, what many Americans call soccer is actually called football in other countries.

Crash and Mike DeLuca love to play football. Crash hopes to score more touchdowns than any player on his team. He may be good at sports, but he is not very good at resolving conflicts between himself and other people. Crash might benefit from creating his own personal playbook—a chart showing the process involved in carrying out various offensive and defensive plays in the game of football.

Materials

- lined paper
- pencils
- a three-ring notebook

Directions

1. Get into groups of four. Assign one person to be the writer. Then, select a scene from *Crash* that depicts conflict.
2. Assign students a role in the scene. Practice acting out that scene.
3. Discuss how the conflict may be solved. Think about how each character could react, and what he/she could say in order to avoid conflict. Chart your suggestions down on a piece of paper, following the model, below. Act out your new, improved scene.
4. Now, act out the original scene for your class. Read your suggestions for solving the conflict.
5. Finally, act out the new scene, demonstrating how the characters work to resolve their conflicts.
6. Collect each group's page and create a "Conflict Resolution Playbook" for your classroom.

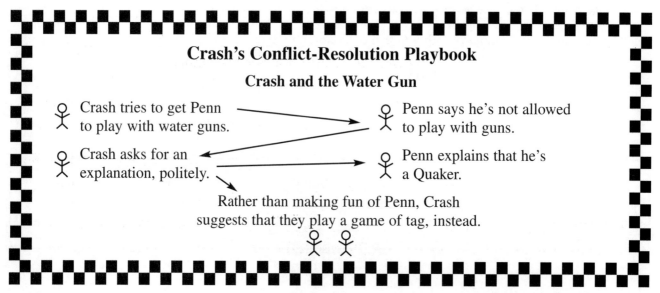

Crash's Conflict-Resolution Playbook
Crash and the Water Gun

Crash tries to get Penn to play with water guns. → Penn says he's not allowed to play with guns.

Crash asks for an explanation, politely. ← Penn explains that he's a Quaker.

Rather than making fun of Penn, Crash suggests that they play a game of tag, instead.

Substituting Synonyms

Crash learns many new and interesting concepts throughout the novel. Likewise, the book is full of new and exciting vocabulary words. The activity below will help you understand words which appear in Section 1.

Synonyms are two or more words that have the same meaning. For instance, a synonym for *dog* is *canine*, and a synonym for *flower* is *blossom*. Using what you've learned about the vocabulary words in Section 1, rewrite each sentence below. Substitute a vocabulary word from the box as a synonym for each bolded word or phrase.

Synonyms	
pestering	consume
vegetarian	violence
scrawny	glum
bamboozled	misery

1. Penn Webb wears a button on his _____ chest.
   (skinny)

2. A Quaker is someone who does not believe in _____ .
   (fighting)

3. Crash feels _____ when Penn almost beats him in a race.
   (tricked)

4. Penn looks _____ after Crash says he won't go to his house for dinner.
   (sad)

5. Penn is a _____ .
   (person who does not eat meat)

6. The Webbs believe people should not _____ animals.
   (eat)

7. Crash appears to be in _____ after he bites into the oatburger.
   (despair)

8. In third grade, Penn stops _____ Crash to go places with him.
   (harassing)

Who Would You Be: Crash or Penn?

Who would you rather be—Crash Coogan or Penn Webb? The two boys are very different from one another. Do you admire one more than the other? Reread the first section of *Crash*, and then complete a Venn Diagram to help you compare and contrast the two main characters. A few character traits have been filled in for you.

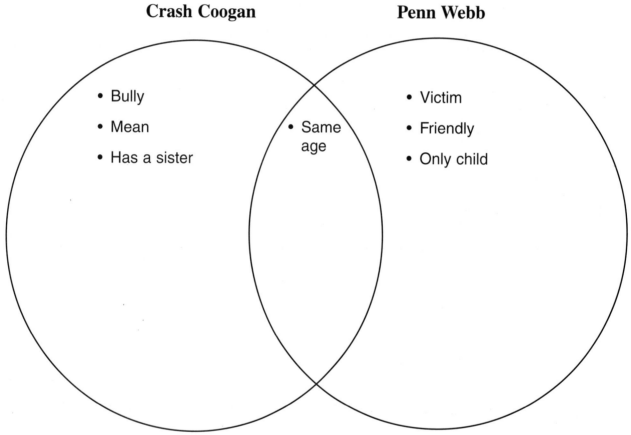

Crash Coogan

- Bully
- Mean
- Has a sister

- Same age

Penn Webb

- Victim
- Friendly
- Only child

Discuss the differences between the two characters with other students and your teacher. Now, write a journal entry about which character you would rather be. Support your opinion with specific details from the story.

Finally, determine how many students in your class would prefer to be like Crash and how many would prefer to be like Penn. Discuss the results.

Quiz Time

Answer the following questions about chapters 9–18.

1. What does Crash think about wearing clothes from a thrift shop?

    _____

    _____

2. What leads to the lunchroom fight between Crash and Mike?

    _____

    _____

3. Why is Crash shocked when he sees who is going out for cheerleading?

    _____

    _____

4. How is Abby different from her brother, Crash?

    _____

    _____

5. How do Crash and Mike bully Penn?

    _____

    _____

6. Why does Abby refuse to eat pepperoni?

    _____

    _____

7. How do Crash's parents act when they come home from work?

    _____

    _____

8. Why does Jane Forbes glare at Crash during the football game?

    _____

    _____

Create a Comic Strip

In Chapter 16, Crash and Mike discover a mouse in the kitchen. Crash is so nervous that he leaps up on the table! Reread this chapter, and create a mental image of what the characters look like and act like in this scene. Then create a comic strip, capturing the characters' feelings, actions, and emotions as they see the mouse running across the kitchen floor.

Make extra copies of the strip as needed.

Reduce, Reuse, Recycle

Penn gets his clothes at Second Time Around, a thrift shop. When Abby asks what a thrift shop is, Crash answers, "Used. Like in used clothes. He wears rags that other people throw away." In actuality, Penn does not wear rags. He wears clothes that other people have donated to the thrift shop as part of an effort to reduce waste and reuse and recycle good clothing.

There are many reasons that people try to reduce, reuse, and recycle objects. The "Three Rs," as they're called, help to conserve energy and natural resources. They help reduce the garbage in landfills, and they can keep product costs down.

See how many creative uses you can think of for common household items that you might otherwise throw away!

Directions

Get into groups of four. Together, fill out the chart below. Consider each object, and all of its various uses. Study the example below for ideas. When your chart is complete, share it with your classmates.

Object	Creative Uses
Shoebox	Cover it with colored paper and use it for a postage stamp, photo, or baseball card collection. Wrap the box and the lid separately in wrapping paper to make a reusable gift box.
Egg Carton	
Rubber Band	
Paper Bag	
One Sock	
Birthday Card	

The Football-Math Connection

In the novel, Crash Coogan and Mike DeLuca are both on the football team. They may have to figure out some math problems in order to become better players. See if you can solve the following stories for them. Make a T-chart to solve the math stories. On one side put your work. On the other side, state your explanation.

work	explanation

1. The score against Hillside is 42–12. If a touchdown is worth six points and a field goal is worth three points, write five different combinations the teams could get to equal a 42–12 total game score.

2. The school football team practices every weekday. Crash ran 25 yards for a touchdown at Monday's practice, 30 yards at Tuesday's practice, and 35 yards at Wednesday's practice. If he continues with this pattern, how many yards will he run for each of his next five practices? Explain the pattern.

3. About 500 people attended the game against Hillside. If each ticket was priced at $2.50, how much money did the school take in? Explain your answer.

4. Mike and Crash competed for the most touchdowns scored. Crash made ½ of the 112 touchdowns scored and Mike made ¼ of the touchdowns. How many touchdowns did each boy score? What was the percentage of touchdowns scored by each boy? Explain your answers.

5. Penn purchased his cheerleading outfit at Second Time Around clothing store. If he paid 25% less than at retail price, how much did Penn pay for each item?

Item	Retail Price	Penn Paid
Shirt	$18.00	
Pants	$35.00	
Socks	$4.00	
Belt	$6.00	
Shoes	$25.00	

What was the total amount that Penn saved? Explain your answers.

Believe in Yourself

Penn Webb seems to rise above the bullying that Crash and Mike inflict upon him. He ignores their actions. No matter what they say or do, he still continues to believe in himself and his values.

In Chapter 14, Crash and Mike put a "Pinch Me" sign on Penn's back and hide his belongings. One day, they put mustard in Penn's sneakers. Penn simply takes off his shoes and walks down the hall in yellow socks.

Activities

1. Break into groups of four. Using newspapers, magazines, and/or movies, find one example of bullying. Answer the following questions:

   - Who is doing the bullying? Who is being bullied?

   - What happens as a result of this bullying?

   - What advice would you give the bully?

   - What advice would you give the person who is being bullied?

2. In your groups, study the chart below. On the left side, read examples of students being bullied. On the right side, list suggestions for helping those students to believe in themselves and stay true to their values.

Conflict	Suggestions
A bully challenges another student to a fight.	The student can say no. If this doesn't work, tell the teacher or enlist help from the school principal.
A bully steals a student's lunch money.	
A bully laughs at a student's clothes.	
A bully hides a student's school books.	
A bully calls a student bad names.	

Quiz Time

1. Who visits Crash, and why is Crash so excited about the visit?

   _____

   _____

2. What routine do Crash, Abby, and Scooter enact before going to bed?

   _____

   _____

3. Why does Crash dance with a sixth-grade student?

   _____

   _____

4. How does Jane Forbes react when Crash asks her to dance?

   _____

   _____

5. Who does Jane end up dancing with? How does this make Crash feel?

   _____

   _____

6. Who are the "mall stallers"?

   _____

   _____

7. How does Crash's mother react to Abby's appearance on the evening news?

   _____

   _____

8. Why does Crash tackle his grandfather?

   _____

   _____

Making Protest Posters

In *Crash*, Abby, Jane, and Penn protest the building of a new mall by creating buttons, T-shirts, and posters which urge people to preserve the land for animals and their habitat. Research an issue that you feel strongly about and make a poster that demonstrates your concern for this issue.

Materials

- current newspapers or periodicals
- blank paper
- pencils
- poster board
- markers or paint and paintbrushes
- stickers
- old magazines
- scissors
- glue

Directions

1. Read current newspapers to find controversial events and issues. Pay particular attention to editorial pages and local news sections. Identify an issue that you feel strongly about.

2. Ask your teacher to approve your issue.

3. Choose a position either for or against the issue.

4. Sketch an idea for your poster on blank paper. Think of images and slogans that will persuade people to see your side of an issue.

5. Create your poster. Use markers or paints, as well as colorful stickers and pictures from magazines to catch people's attention.

6. Present your poster to the class and share information about your issue.

	Example Issue
○	
	The local City Council is going to ban skateboarding in a nearby park,
	because it disturbs visitors. This topic is controversial, because kids in the
○	neighborhood have been asked not to skateboard around public buildings and
	parking lots. The park is the only place in which they are permitted to
	skateboard freely. If officials forbid skateboarding in the park, the
	skateboarders will have no place to go.
○	**Save Our Skateboards!**

Pennsylvania and North Dakota

Penn tells Crash that he moved from North Dakota to Pennsylvania. What are the differences between these two states? What are their similarities?

Get into groups of four. Visit your school's library and make use of the reference section. Study almanacs, atlases, encyclopedias, and the Internet to research each state. Then, compare the states to one another.

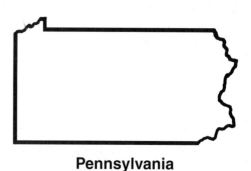

Pennsylvania

Topics	Pennsylvania	North Dakota
Population		
Size		
Climate		
Geography		
State Capital		
Points of Interest		
State Flag		
State Flower		
State Bird		
State's Nickname		

North Dakota

Finally, choose one state and create a tourism brochure with your group. Include the above information, as well as a map highlighting points of interest for tourists. You can illustrate the brochures with drawings, photocopies of reference materials, and/or downloaded pictures from the Internet.

What is a Quaker?

In the novel, Penn informs Crash that he is a Quaker. Crash regards this with suspicion, as Quakers seem very different from him. Use the Internet, encyclopedias, books, and other resources to answer the following questions about Quakers and their history.

1. What is a Quaker? _____

   _____

2. What are their beliefs? _____

   _____

3. Are there any famous Quakers? _____

   _____

4. How did Quakers get their name? _____

   _____

5. How does this information help you to understand Penn and his family? _____

   _____

Now, prepare to write a one-page report on Quakers. An outline will help you to organize your paper effectively. Fill in the blanks below to complete your outline.

Topic: Quakers

I. Paragraph One—Introduction

  A. Main Idea— _____

  1. Supporting Details— _____

II. Paragraph Two—Body

  A. Main Idea— _____

  1. Supporting Details— _____

III. Paragraph Three—Body

  A. Main Idea— _____

  1. Supporting Details— _____

IV. Paragraph Four—Body

  A. Main Idea— _____

  1. Supporting Details— _____

V. Paragraph Five—Conclusion

  A. Main Idea— _____

  1. Supporting Details— _____

Character Motivation

In Chapter 26, Abby and her mother have a fight. Crash hears them through his sister's closed door. The characters have very different passions, or motivations, that drive them to do and say particular things. Through their dialogue, readers can tell that Abby's actions are motivated by a desire to save land and animals. Her mother's actions are motivated by making sure her children have a good life.

> ABBY: Don't you want to save the earth?

> MOM: I want to make a good home for my children, that's what I want."

Think about a time when you fought with one of your parents about an important issue. Write it in play form, like the argument between Abby and her mother. In your play, make sure that the reader understands both characters and their motivations.

Quiz Time

1. What has happened to Scooter?

   _____

   _____

2. Why does Crash get upset when Mike walks into the bedroom wearing a sailor hat?

   _____

   _____

3. Why does Crash buy a pair of shoes for Scooter?

   _____

   _____

4. Why does Crash make catfish cakes for Abby?

   _____

   _____

5. How does Crash act when Mike brings the Jetwater Uzi to school?

   _____

   _____

6. After reading Penn's essay, what do you think Penn and Crash have in common?

   _____

   _____

7. How does Crash react when he discovers Penn's turtle in Mike's bedroom closet?

   _____

   _____

8. What is Abby doing to try and make the backyard into a wildlife habitat?

   _____

   _____

Build a Wildlife Habitat

Abby wants to build a backyard habitat for wildlife. This type of habitat offers a combination of food, water, shelter, and space that attracts birds, butterflies, insects, and small animals. Trees and bushes provide shelter and food for wildlife. You can create your own habitat in a corner of your schoolyard, or in a vacant lot.

Consider adopting a piece of land with your classmates and turning it into a welcoming area for wildlife! Below, you'll find important details to remember when building your habitat.

Birds

Many species of birds are attracted to different types of food in different types of feeders. Some prefer feeders that hang from branches or stands. Other birds eat right off the ground. Sunflower seeds appeal to many birds. Woodpeckers, nuthatches, and chickadees love blocks of suet hung from branches. Robins and mockingbirds will flock to citrus, chopped apples, bananas, and raisins. Don't forget to place a shallow dish of water in your habitat for use as a bird bath!

Butterflies

Butterflies get nectar from flowers. The types of flowering plants you grow will determine the kinds of butterflies you attract to your habitat. Butterfly bush is especially appealing. Find out what species of butterflies are common in your area and plant the flowering bushes they prefer. Nectar feeders will also attract butterflies.

Butterflies are active on sunny, warm days. Provide a light-colored rock or concrete garden sculpture as a basking site. Butterflies also need a source of water. A shallow dish of water or a depression in a rock that retains water makes a perfect drinking area.

Reptiles and Amphibians

Most toads, frogs, lizards, turtles, and snakes are harmless and beneficial creatures who feed on destructive insects and rodents. Shelter for reptiles and amphibians is easy to provide. A pile of rocks in a sunny spot becomes a fine basking site. You can plant shade-tolerant groundcovers under trees and leave a thick layer of leaves on the ground to provide cool shelter. Reptiles and amphibians also enjoy stumps, logs, and rock piles in a shady spot.

Backyard Habitat Programs

The National Wildlife Federation (NWF) sponsors a certification program designed to help people plan and create a wildlife habitat plan. NWF will send you an application package and instructions for its Backyard Wildlife Habitat Program. For more information, write to:

Backyard Wildlife Habitat Program
National Wildlife Federation
8925 Leesburg Pike
Vienna, VA 22184-0001

Catfish Cakes

Scooter likes to bake "catfish cakes" for Abby's birthday, but after his stroke, he is too sick. Instead, Crash bakes catfish cakes for his sister in Mike Deluca's microwave oven.

> "Catfish cakes are mostly just regular brownies. What Scooter would do then was make catfish faces by squeezing a string of white icing onto each one."

You can make your own catfish cakes, and then have a classroom contest to determine the best faces.

Materials

- an oven or microwave
- packaged brownie mix
- eggs
- vegetable oil
- chocolate chips (optional)
- baking bowls
- baking pans
- potholders
- spoons
- tubes of white icing
- knife

Note to Teacher: If ovens are not available, pre-bake brownies and bring them for students to decorate and eat. Be sure to assess the class for food allergies and special diets.

Directions

1. Get into groups of four.

2. Preheat oven and prepare brownie batter according to directions on the box. You may choose to add chocolate chips to the batter.

3. Pour batter into greased pans and bake according to the directions on the box.

4. When the brownies are finished baking, let them cool for at least twenty minutes. Then cut them into squares.

5. Distribute one brownie to each student for decoration. Create catfish faces on your brownies with white icing.

6. Display the decorated brownies on a plate and vote for your favorite catfish cake. You might choose to vote for Funniest Face, Scariest Face, and Most Artistic Face.

7. Eat and enjoy your finished catfish cakes!

Scene Visualization

Many of the scenes described by Jerry Spinelli paint a vivid picture in the reader's mind. Illustrating these scenes will increase your understanding of this section.

Materials

- notebook paper
- drawing or watercolor paper
- markers
- crayons
- colored pencils
- watercolor paints
- pastels

Directions

1. Read the activity choices below. Choose one scene to illustrate.

2. Re-read the passages carefully for your chosen scene, paying attention to the pictures you form in your mind as you read.

3. Describe the scene in your own words on notebook paper.

4. Draw or paint a picture that illustrates your chosen scene.

5. Read the scene and share your illustration with the class.

Scene Choices

- In Chapter 32, what does Crash see when he looks out of his bedroom window to find Scooter sitting on the ground? Describe the scene in your own words after reading the passage that starts with "It happened last Saturday…" through "…the siren that sounded like a kazoo going farther away." Draw or paint a picture that matches this scene.

- Compare the Coogan's family Christmas tree to the one Crash imagines he will have in his own apartment some day. Read Chapter 32, starting with "Like every year, the Christmas tree stands in the corner of the living room . . ." to ". . . around the tree like a mummy." Draw or paint a picture to match the description of each tree.

- When Crash feels depressed about Scooter's condition, he takes a walk, then wanders into his own backyard. Read the passage in Chapter 35 that begins with "As backyards go, ours is pretty big . . ." to the end of the chapter. Draw or paint a picture to illustrate this scene.

- When Mike leaves school with his Jetwater Uzi, Crash does not go with him. Read the passage in Chapter 36 that begins "This afternoon, a block from school, a gang of kids…" through ". . . the shots would ping off the stop sign." Draw or paint the scene, including as many of Jerry Spinelli's descriptive details in the passage as you can.

What You Mean to Me

In Chapter 39 of the novel, Crash and his classmates get an English assignment. "Write an essay about someone you know. Tell what that person means to you." Crash writes about Scooter and how he cooks, plays games, tells stories, and attends his football games. Penn write about his great-grandfather, too. He wants his great-grandfather to see him competing in the Penn Relays.

Think about someone you know well. Consider what that person means to you. In the space below, write a short essay about that person, using specific details. You may choose to outline your essay first, using the outline described on page 23.

Quiz Time

1. How does the coach select the team for the Penn Relays?

   _____

   _____

2. Why does Crash's mother change her work schedule?

   _____

   _____

3. What happens during the race-off for the spot to run in the Penn Relays?

   _____

   _____

4. How does Penn help the team in the Penn Relays?

   _____

   _____

5 Why does Scooter climb the stairs?

   _____

   _____

6. What does Crash spend his sneaker money on, and why?

   _____

   _____

7. How do Crash's parents change during the course of this novel?

   _____

   _____

8. How does Crash change during the course of this novel?

   _____

   _____

Family Portrait

When Crash and Abby find out that their mother has cut back on her work hours, they are excited. Finally, she will spend time with them!

Abby wants Mom to paint portraits again. Crash uses his sneaker money to buy her a set of paints.

You can also create a family portrait for Crash and Abby. Think about what each character looks like. You may need to go through the book once more to refresh your memory. Then create a tissue paper portrait of Crash, Abby, their parents, and Scooter.

Materials

- one sheet of white construction paper for each student
- colored tissue paper, cut or torn into 1' (2.54 cm) squares
- glue
- colored construction paper
- index cards
- pencils

Directions

1. Draw an outline of Crash's family on white paper.

2. Grasp the center of one tissue paper square and twist the paper to form a rosette. Place a dab of glue on the bottom of the rosette and press it onto the white paper.

3. Fill in the rest of your outline with tissue paper rosettes.

4. Create a frame for your portrait out of colored construction paper.

5. On an index card, write the title of your portrait and a short description of the characters.

6. Create a gallery of portraits on your classroom wall.

Act It Out!

One way to experience literature is by acting it out. Great books are often adapted into plays or movies. Dramatizing books can be enjoyable and interesting. You can bring *Crash* to life by writing scripts and performing scenes from the novel.

Directions

1. Work in groups of two to four students.

2. Skim through the novel to select an event for your script.

3. Write a script for your chosen event. Add dialogue and narration, as well as setting details.

4. Assign each student a role, and try to memorize your script.

5. Create a stage at the front of your classroom, and set it with appropriate props.

6. Act out the scene for your class.

Script Example:

The following example is from chapter 45. Crash comes home from school to find his mom there.

Characters:

- Crash
- Crash's mother

(Crash walks through the door.)

Crash: (Acting surprised.) You sick?

Crash's mom: No, just home.

Crash: You got fired?

Crash's mom: (chuckling) I quit. Actually, I half quit. I will work part-time from now on. I need to take care of Scooter. Now, would you rather have the money or my time?

Crash: Your money.

Crash's mom: I knew I shouldn't have asked.

Crash: But what about Mrs. Linfont?

Crash's mom: She got fired. So that means I'll be making dinner tonight.

Crash: Not good.

(Crash's mom laughs.)

Other Performance Ideas

- Make props and costumes appropriate for your scene.
- Videotape your performance to create a *Crash* movie.
- Instead of acting out the scenes, you may create puppets and put on a puppet show.
- Perform your scenes for other classrooms.

Compose a Cinquain

Crash spends a great deal of time bullying Penn. However, at the end of the story, the boys put their past differences aside and became good friends. This is only possible because Crash stops being a bully.

A *cinquain* is an American form of poetry, five lines long. Write a cinquain to show the effects of bullying on a victim, or to show reasons to stop bullying.

Study the pattern for a cinquain and the example to the right.

Line 1 title (*noun*)

Line 2 description of title (*two adjectives*)

Line 3 action of title (*three verbs*)

Line 4 statement or feeling (*four-word phrase*)

Line 5 repeated title or synonym (*noun*)

Cinquain Example
bully
mean, evil
teasing, destroying, haunting
makes you feel lifeless
bully

Now, write your cinquain in the space below. You may choose to copy it on heavy paper and add a collage of pictures that illustrate the message of your poem. Share your collage and cinquain with your classmates.

_____

_____

_____

_____

_____

Family Stew

Crash and Abby used to feel safe when they climbed into Scooter's bed and listened to stories. After his stroke, their feelings change. Now that Scooter can no longer tell his life stories to Crash and Abby, they must take on the role of captain and tell him stories of their own.

Every family has a story to tell. It may be a story about relatives, friends, or adventures. Whenever you hear someone's personal story, you are participating in oral history. Usually, this story is not written down, but is passed from one generation to another through storytelling, just as Scooter does when he tells his stories to Crash and Abby.

You can create a Family Stew Bag for your family stories.

Directions

1. Ask older friends or relatives to tell you their personal stories. Prepare some questions to keep the conversation going. Here are a few suggestions. Feel free to add your own questions.

   - Tell me a humorous story from your past.

   - Tell me about our family history.

   - When did our family immigrate to this country?

   - How are things different now from when you were young?

   - Did you serve our country? Tell me a story about your service time.

   - What are some traditions we do as a family and how did they get started?

   - What did you do for fun when you were younger?

2. Now that you know your family's history, collect items or pictures to help you remember these stories. Place these items into a "Family Stew" bag. Each item should represent a different story about your family. Items may include models, symbols, pictures, computer graphics, or pictures from magazines. For example, if you were telling a story about your family immigrating to the United States via boat, you might include a model of a boat to help you tell this story.

3. Once you have compiled your Family Stew, practice telling your family's stories at home.

4. Finally, share one family story with your classmates and teacher.

Any Questions?

When you finished reading *Crash*, did you have any questions that were left unanswered? Write your questions here.

1. _____

2. _____

3. _____

Work in groups or by yourself to prepare possible answers for some or all of the questions you have asked above and for those written below. When you have finished, share your predictions with the class.

- Does Scooter ever make a full recovery?

- How do Penn and Crash become good friends?

- Do Jane and Penn ever go out on a date?

- Do Jane and Crash ever go out on a date?

- Does Crash lead the football team to a championship?

- Does Crash's mom pursue her art?

- What is the first portrait that Crash's mom paints with her new set of paints?

- Do Crash and his dad ever go to a Phillies' game?

- Are Crash and Mike still friends?

- What stories do Abby and Crash tell Scooter about?

- Did Crash really let Penn win the relay race?

- What happens at the Penn Relays in eighth grade?

- How does Abby's backyard habitat turn out?

- Will Mike stop being a bully now?

- Will the Coogan family be able to get by without the extra money Mrs. Coogan earned?

- Does the mall get built or do the Mall Stallers stop it?

- What careers do Crash, Abby, Mike, Jane, and Penn choose?

Book Report Ideas

There are many ways to report on a book. After completing *Crash*, choose a method of reporting on the story. Pick from the list below or choose your own idea.

- **Add a Chapter**

  Add a chapter to *Crash*. The chapter can take place within the story or afterwards. Make sure you are telling the story from Crash's point of view.

- **Book Review**

  Write a book review about *Crash*. A book review states your reaction or opinion about the book. Make sure you support your opinion with specific facts and details from the story.

- **Design a Book Cover**

  Design a book cover for the novel. Include the title; author; and an important scene, image, or character on the front cover. Include a book summary on the inside cover and a teaser on the back.

- **Design a CD Cover**

  Suppose the book was going to become a musical. Include the title, author, and an image on the front cover. On the back cover, include a list of possible song titles that could be on this CD (the titles may be real songs or made up). On the inside flaps, write a song that summarizes the story.

- **Act it Out**

  Act out your favorite scene from the book with your classmates. Have each member create costumes and props to assist. Afterwards, relate the significance of the scene to the entire book.

- **An Oral Report**

  Summarize your favorite parts of the book and be sure to give reasons why you feel that way.

- **Create a Board Game**

  Create a board game for the story. Create question cards for the game that can be answered from reading the book. You might model it after board games you play at home or in the classroom.

- **Design a Scrapbook**

  Use magazine pictures, photographs, and other illustrations to create a scrapbook that Crash might keep to document his life. He might choose to decorate his scrapbook with stickers, or include football programs and his mother's portraits.

- **Design a Diorama**

  Using a shoebox as a frame, create a diorama that illustrates an important scene in the novel. You may use paper, sand, clay, paint, fabric, etc., to bring this scene to life.

36

Research Ideas

As you read *Crash*, you discovered geographical locations, events, and people about which you might wish to know more. To increase your understanding of the characters, places, and events in this novel, do research to find out additional information.

Work alone or in groups to find out more about one or more of the items listed below. You may use books, magazines, and the Internet to conduct your research. Afterwards, share your findings with the class.

- football
- backyard habitats
- political protests
- strokes
- thrift stores
- the Penn Relays
- Quakers
- North Dakota
- Pennsylvania
- box turtles
- vegetarians
- cheerleading
- the effects of bullying
- portrait painting
- oral history
- cooking
- running
- garage sales
- therapeutic mud
- Jerry Spinelli
- Flickertail squirrels
- mice in your house

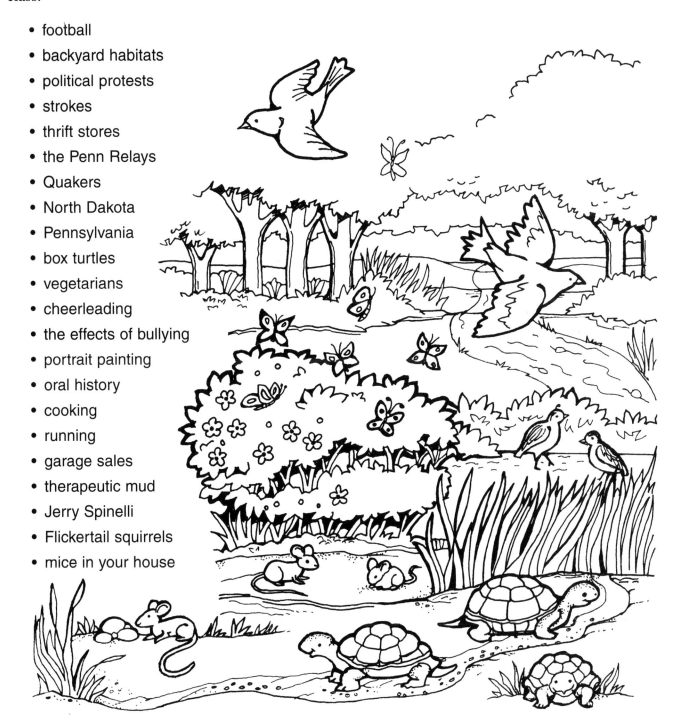

The Crash Bag

For a greater understanding of *Crash*, fill an ordinary brown paper bag with objects and pictures that have specific meaning to the novel. The bag can be decorated and labeled. Display one item at a time. Ask students to discuss what each item means in the story.

Here are suggested items to include in your *Crash* Bag.

- Quaker Oats oatmeal box
- Box from vegetarian burgers
- Jar of mud or dirt
- Protest sign
- Protest button
- Women's red high-heeled shoes
- USA map
- Running shoes
- Football helmet
- Brownie Mix
- Hospital bracelet
- Real estate business card
- Protest T-shirt
- Baseball cap
- Model of a Conestoga wagon
- Plastic mouse

- Gym bag
- Lawnmower
- Dollhouse
- Sailor's cap
- Balled up piece of notebook paper
- Turtle
- Christmas tree
- Family portrait
- Packet of mustard
- Plastic squirt gun
- Bird feeder
- Frozen pizza box
- Coupons
- Garage-sale sign
- Item of clothing from thrift store

Note to Teacher: You may also ask students to bring in a designated number of objects to place in the *Crash* bag, along with a written explanation for each. Or, have them create and display their own *Crash* Bag.

Character Report Card

Choose three characters from the story. Assign a grade to the characters based on their traits in the beginning of the story and one based on traits shown at the end of the story. Look at how your chosen characters have changed. Write comments about how you think these characters have grown or not grown, based on specific scenes from the novel.

Report Card

Character's Name _____

Role in the story _____

Behavior	Beginning Grade	Ending Grade	Comments	Example
Kind				
Athletic				
Polite				
Mature				
Understanding				
Competitive				

A = all of the time	C = sometimes
B = frequently	D = never

Reader's Theater

In *Crash*, readers learn that bullying hurts people, but bullies can change. Use Reader's Theater to further explore this theme.

Materials

- fabric paint
- markers
- paper
- pencils
- scissors
- plain T-shirts
- buttons
- butcher paper

Directions

Part I: Creating a T-shirt and a Button

1. Ask students to think of slogans to promote positive relationships. Record students' suggestions on butcher paper.

2. Ask students to design a T-shirt or a button using one or more of the brainstormed slogans. For example, they might use "Stop bullying! Solve conflicts peacefully."

Part II: Reader's Theater Skit

1. Form groups of three to five students. Ask students to wear buttons and T-shirts when performing their skit.

2. Each group should write a skit about a child who goes through one day receiving all negative comments. Then have students write a second skit showing a child's day full of positive comments.

Part III: Creating a Paper Character

1. Ask a student from each group to lie down on a long piece of butcher paper. Trace the outline of the student's body.

2. Cut the "body" out for a life-sized paper doll to use as a paper character.

Part IV: Performing the Skit

1. Groups should select one student to read one of the skits, one student to hold the paper doll, and other students to take each role in the skit.

2. Have the students perform the skit with the negative comments. As the character receives each negative comment, the student holding the paper character will crumble part of it. At the end of the skit, the paper doll should be crumpled into a ball.

3. Have the students perform the skit with the positive comments. Each time a positive comment is read, have the student holding the paper doll unfold part of it. At the end of this skit, the paper doll should be uncrumpled.

4. Lead the students in a discussion about how the wrinkles in the paper character are still visible— the same way the effects of bullying can remain with an individual forever.

Party Time!

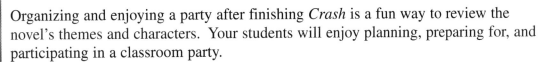

Organizing and enjoying a party after finishing *Crash* is a fun way to review the novel's themes and characters. Your students will enjoy planning, preparing for, and participating in a classroom party.

Party Checklist

Three weeks before the party . . .

- Decide on a date, time, and place for your party.
- Think of a theme for your party. Themes related to this book include wildlife habitats, football, Thanksgiving, families, and running.
- Decide whether your class wants to invite guests to the party. Will you invite family members? Other classrooms? Make and send the invitations on the next page.
- Discuss decorations. Will you use the paper dolls from page 11, scene visualizations from page 28, family portraits from page 31, or cinquain-collages from page 33?

Two weeks before the party . . .

- Decide what food and/or drink you will make as a class. This book provides ideas for Catfish Cakes on page 27. You might serve vegetarian burgers, frozen pizzas, or another food related to the novel. Make a grocery list.
- Pass around a sign-up sheet. Each student should be encouraged to bring something unique to the party. They might bring food, sign up to play musical instruments or demonstrate sports, bring a favorite small pet, or tell a family story. Perhaps your students will give tours of their new wildlife habitat from page 26, perform their skits from page 32, or act out Reader's Theater from page 40.
- Send home a note to students' parents to let them know the date and time of the party, as well as what the student signed up to bring.

One week before the party . . .

- Send home a note reminding students of what they are to bring for the party.
- Buy and/or make decorations.

The day before the party . . .

- Make any chosen snacks.

The day of the party . . .

- Decorate the party space.
- Finish making any chosen snacks and drinks.
- Have fun!

Party Time! *(oont.)*

Students should color and write on the invitation below to invite guests to their Crash Party. Duplicate as many copies of this page as needed. Then cut around the border.

You're invited!

What: _____

Who: _____

When: _____

Where: _____

Why: _____

42

Objective Test and Essay

Matching: Match the descriptions of each character with their names.

1. Crash Coogan

2. Penn Webb

3. Abby Coogan

4. Scooter

5. Mike DeLuca

6. Jane Forbes

7. Mrs. Coogan

8. Mr. Coogan

9. Mr. and Mrs. Webb

10. Penn's great-grandfather

a. ran in the Penn Relays in 1919

b. bakes catfish cakes and tells stories

c. used to be a bully, but now he's kind

d. wants to turn her backyard into a wildlife habitat

e. vegetarians who don't own a television

f. too busy with work to take his son to a baseball game

g. helps Penn and Abby to stall the mall

h. very proud of his new Jetwater Uzi and sneakers

i. cuts back her work hours to spend time with the family

j. doesn't let bullying stop him from helping the world

True or False: Answer **true** or **false** in the blanks below.

_____ 1. Crash got his nickname from knocking over his cousin.

_____ 2. Mike DeLuca admires and likes Penn Webb.

_____ 3. Jane Forbes does not like Crash's over-confident attitude.

_____ 4. Scooter recovers fully from his stroke.

_____ 5. Crash and Penn end up being best friends.

Short Answer: Write a brief response on separate paper.

1. How are Penn's and Crash's families different?

2. What common values do Penn, Abby, and Jane share? How can you tell?

3. After Crash tackles Scooter, he tries to reason with himself about his motives for his actions. Why do you think Crash tacked his grandfather? Explain your answer.

4. Before the race-off begins, Crash pictures a gift for Penn's great-grandfather. What is the gift and how does Crash help to give the gift?

Essay: Respond to the following on a separate piece of paper.

Throughout most of the story, Crash is annoyed or irritated by Penn and his actions. By the end of the story, Penn is Crash's best friend. Explain how and why Crash changes his attitude toward Penn.

Quotations

On a separate sheet of paper, explain the meaning of each of these quotations from Crash.

Chapter 3: "I was almost starting to enjoy this kid, like I was the cat and he was my mouse."

Chapter 6: "We're not poor at all. In fact, I would say in a lot of ways we're rich."

Chapter 8: "Mike looked out the window again. It was like watching a cat watching a squirrel. 'Well,' he said, 'that's gonna change.'"

Chapter 13: "Whoopee. Just like a real family."

Chapter 20: "We both grew up thinking Scooter's bed was the safest place in the world, like a boat in a sea full of crocs."

Chapter 26: "I mean, one of the reasons why your father and I work so long and hard is so you don't have to wear second hand clothes."

Chapter 30: "But now sleeping in the bed of my ten-year-old sister, on her Sylvester sheets and Tweety pillowcase, he was just about as old as anybody I ever saw. I didn't like it."

Chapter 32: "The register pinged, and a sign saying ten dollars shot up. I took my first breath of the morning. I took the bag from the lady. I closed my eyes, and I swear I saw, or felt, right at that moment something dark and ugly and bottomless back away from a certain hospital door in Springfield."

Chapter 36: "Was Mike right? Was I a dud? Why wasn't I joining the mob and hooting with the rest of them? Why wasn't I grabbing the gun and pumping a couple of rounds into the victim myself?"

Chapter 37: "Let's try to concentrate on what he can do,' said my mom, 'not on what he can't."

Chapter 44: "Boys, we have our own little Penn Relays tradition here at Springfield. I don't especially care whether we win or not. I've been taking teams to the Penn Relays for sixteen years now, and we've never won the suburban middle school race, not once, and I intend to continue that perfect record."

Chapter 49: "We're going to a ball game! My mother got the tickets. Five of them for herself, Scooter, Abby, me, and my father. He says he won't have time to go. My mom says he'll be there. Abby bet me a water ice that my mom will win. I said my dad. Hope I lose."

Conversations

Work in groups to write the conversations that might have occurred between the people in the following situations. Then perform your conversation for the class.

- Crash's mother catches her son digging up pansies in the garden. (*2 people*)

- Crash meets Penn for the first time, and he invites Penn to dig in the garden with him. (*2 people*)

- Crash's father wakes him up to discuss the Phillies game and agrees to take Crash and the family to the game on Saturday. (*2 people*)

- Crash tells his family about his visit to Penn's house for dinner. (*3–4 people*)

- Penn stands up to Crash and Mike when he finds out they have put mustard into his sneakers during geography class. (*3 people*)

- Jane Forbes helps Penn wash out his sneakers after Crash and Mike put the mustard into them. (*2 people*)

- Jane Forbes agrees to dance with Crash, not Penn, at the school dance. (*2–4 people*)

- Penn introduces his great-grandfather, Henry Wilhide Webb III, to Crash's grandfather, Scooter. (*4 people*)

- Abby and Crash tell Scooter bedtime stories when he comes home from the hospital. (*3 people*)

- Abby, Penn, and Jane share the news that the new mall will not be built. (*3 or more people*)

- The vice-principal suspends Mike and Crash when he hears about the food fight in the cafeteria. (*3 people*)

- Crash Coogan's parents go to the football game to see him score his six touchdowns, then take him for ice cream after the game. (*3 people*)

- When Abby asks Crash to build the observation tower in the backyard, he agrees to do it if she helps him. (*2 people*)

- Scooter is able to talk to them when they visit him after the stroke. (*3 people*)

- Crash gets the sneakers he wanted for Christmas, and he shows them to Mike. (*2 people*)

- Crash answers the door when Penn Webb delivers the Missouri River mud jar for Scooter. (*2 or 3 people*)

- Abby is thrilled with the "catfish cakes" that Crash had made for her birthday. (*2 people*)

- Mike understands how Crash feels about Scooter's stroke. (*2 people*)

- Abby's father agrees to help her build a wildlife habitat in their backyard. (*2 people*)

- Crash wins the race-off to see who goes to the Penn Relay Races. (*2 or 3 people*)

- Scooter watches Crash as he lets Penn Webb win the race-off. (*2 people*)

- Crash congratulates Penn Webb for the team's second place trophy from the Penn Relays. (*2 people*)

- Crash talks to Jane Forbes at her Fourth of July party. (*2 people*)

Bibliography of Related Reading

Fiction

Berenstain, J. & Berenstain, S. *The Berenstain Bears and the Bully*. (Random House, 1993)

Carlson, Nancy. *Loudmouth George and the Sixth-Grade Bully*. (Lerner, 2003)

Cole, Joanna. *Bully Trouble. Step into Reading Series: A Step 2 Book*. (Random House, 1989)

Cordon, A. & Cordell, M. *Gorillas of Gill Park*. (Holiday House, 2003)

DeClements, Barthe. *Nothing's Fair in Fifth Grade*. (Viking, 1981)

Hayes, Geoffrey. *Patrick and the Big Bully*. (Hyperion Books for Children, 2001)

Hiaasen, C. *Hoot*. (Random House, 2002)

Martin, Ann M. *Karen's Bully. The Baby-Sitters Club: Little Sister Series #31*. (Scholastic, 1992)

Mayer, Gina & Mercer. *Just a Bully. Little Critter Series*. (Golden Books, 1999)

Naylor Reynolds, Phillis. *King of the Playground*. (Atheneum, 1991)

Pascal, Francine. *Bully. Sweet Valley Twins Series #19*. (Bantam Doubleday Dell Books for Young Readers, 1988)

Resnick, Mike. *Bwana-Bully!* (Doherty, Tome Associates, 1991)

Robinson, Nancy K. *Wendy and the Bullies*. (Hastings House Daytrips Publishers, 1987)

Romain, T. *Bullies are a Pain in the Brain*. (Free Spirit Publishing, 1997)

Schorr, Mark. *Bully!* (St. Martin's Press, 1985)

Stolz, Mary. *The Bully of Brakham Street*. (HarperCollins Children's Books, 1985)

Nonfiction and Teacher Resources

Boulden, Boulden, & Ward. *Playground Push-Around: Bully and Victim Activity Book*. (Boulden, 1994)

Beane, Allen. *The Bully Free Classroom: Over 100 Tips and Strategies for Teachers K-8*. (Free Spirit Publishing, 1999)

Carter, J. & Noll K. *Taking the Bully by the Horns: Children's Version of the Best Selling Book, Nasty People*. (Unicorn Press, 1998)

Cohen-Posey, K. *How to Handle Bullies, Teasers and Other Meanies*. (Rainbow Books, 1995)

Fried, S. & Fried, P. *Bullies and Victims: Helping Your Child Through the Schoolyard Battlefield*. (Evans & Co., 1996)

Gibbons, G. & Jch. *Recycle!: A Handbook for Kids*. (Little Brown and Company, 1996)

Johnson, K. & Yardley, T. *A Worm's Eye View: Making Your Own Wildlife Refuge*. (Millbrook Press, 1992)

Jones, T., Compton, R., O., Randolph. *Kids Working it Out: Stories and Strategies for Making Peace in Our Schools*. (Wiley Imprint, 2003)

Langan, P. *Bullying in Schools: What You Need to Know*. (Townsend Press, 2003)

McNamara, B. & McNamara, F. *Keys to Dealing with Bullies*. (Barron's, 1997)

Paley, V. *You Can't Say You Can't Play*. (Harvard University Press, 1992)

Quinn, K., Barone, B., Kearns, J., Stackhouse, S., & Zimmerman, M. "Using a Novel Unit to Help Understand and Prevent Bullying in Schools." *Journal of Adolescent and Adult Literacy,* 46(7), 582-591.

Answer Key

Page 10

1. Crash gets his nickname when he receives a football helmet for Christmas. When his relatives arrive, Crash charges at them, knocking his cousin out the door and into the snow.

2. Crash is in the yard digging a hole, and Penn walks up the street. He is new to the neighborhood. Crash won't let Penn pass. Penn is polite and introduces himself.

3. Crash's sister tells Penn her brother's real name. Crash is mad because he doesn't get to tell Penn himself.

4. Penn is a Quaker and does not believe in violence.

5. Crash is surprised at how close Penn is behind him because no one has ever come close to beating him.

6. Penn is an only child. His parents are older. They are Quakers and vegetarians with no television.

7. He has just started his own business and does not have time to spend with his family.

8. Mike Deluca is bold and competitive, while Penn is friendly and a pacifist. Mike is a bully, and Penn is his victim.

Page 13

1. scrawny
2. violence
3. bamboozled
4. glum
5. vegetarian
6. consume
7. misery
8. pestering

Page 15

1. Crash thinks that clothes from a thrift shop are disgusting.

2. Arguing over Jane Forbes leads to a fight between Crash and Mike.

3. Crash is shocked to find Penn going out for cheerleading because he doesn't believe boys should be cheerleaders.

4. Abby is loving and gentle, committed to the environment and not harming the earth.

5. Crash and Mike put mustard in Penn's shoes, stick signs on his back, and make fun of him.

6. Abby refuses to eat pepperoni because she's become a vegetarian.

7. Crash's parents are exhausted and bitter when they come home from work.

8. Jane is angry at Crash for being such an aggressive bully during the football game.

Page 18

1. Accept appropriate answers and explanations.

2. Thurs. 40 yards, Fri. 45 yards, Mon. 50 yards, Tues. 55 yards, Wed. 60 yards. Pattern: each day he ran 5 more yards.

3. The school took in $1,250.00.

4. Crash scored 56 touchdowns, which is 50% of the total touchdowns scored. Mike scored 28 touchdowns, which is 25% of the total touchdowns scored.

5. Shirt—$13.50. Pants—$26.25. Socks—$3.00. Belt—$4.50. Shoes—$18.75. Savings—$22.00.

Page 20

1. Scooter comes to visit. Crash is excited because he hasn't seen his grandfather in a while, and Scooter is a good cook and storyteller.

2. They all climb into bed in their pajamas and Scooter tells them stories.

3. The sixth-grader is the first person Crash dances with because Mike DeLuca teases him when Jane ignores him, so Crash grabs the nearest girl with which to dance.

4. Jane refuses to dance with Crash, and when Crash won't leave her alone, she stares coldly and laughs at him. She kicks him, yells at him, and tells him off.

5. Jane dances with Penn. Crash is furious.

6. Penn, Abby, and Jane are the "mall stallers." They sell T-shirts and picket to try to stop the mall from being built.

7. Abby's mother is very upset and wants Abby to stop protesting the mall because she is a real-estate agent, and if the mall isn't built, she will lose money.

8. Crash and Scooter are playing football, and Scooter is about to make a point for his team, so Crash tackles him.

Page 22

Topics	Pennsylvania	North Dakota
Population	12,281,054	642,200
Size	46,058 sq. miles	70,704 sq. miles
Climate	Humid Continental	Continental
Geography	7 Landform Regions	Geographic Center of North America
State Capital	Harrisburg	Bismarck
Points of Interest	Independence Hall, Philadelphia Art Museum, Valley Forge National Park	Sitting Bull's Historic Grove, Theodore Roosevelt National Park
State Flag	Blue background with 2 draft horses surrounding a shield with a ship, a plow and 3 sheaves of wheat. Below is a stalk of corn, an olive branch and a draped red ribbon that reads, "Virtue, Liberty, and Independence."	Blue background, Bald Eagle holding a red ribbon with "E Pluribus Unum." The eagle is holding seven arrows and an olive branch. There are 13 yellow stars and a fan above the eagle and a yellow banner that reads North Dakota below the eagle.
State Flower	Mountain Laurel	White Prairie Rose
State Bird	Ruffed Grouse	Western Meadowlark
State's Nickname	Keystone State	Peace Garden State

Page 25

1. Scooter had a stroke, and he is in the hospital, unable to speak.

Answer Key *(cont.)*

2. Crash gets upset when Mike wears Scooter's hat because he is worried about his grandfather. Crash may feel that no one but Scooter should be in his room, wearing his hat.

3. Crash wants to buy Scooter something as an apology for tackling him. He feels guilty.

4. Crash makes catfish cakes for Abby because he feels sorry for her.

5. Crash tells Mike he's going to get suspended for the Jetwater Uzi, and he and Mike have a fight.

6. Both Scooter and Henry Webb III like to tell stories and enjoy spending time with their grandchildren. Crash and Penn love their grandfathers and admire them.

7. Crash returns Penn's turtle.

8. Abby steals the spark plug from the lawnmower and frightens the ChemLawn man away. She also builds a mouse house.

Page 30

1. The coach holds a race-off to select a runner for the sprinting team.

2. Crash's mother changes her work schedule to care for Scooter and her children.

3. As the race starts, Crash is behind everyone. He closes the gap and near the end of the race, he and Penn are tied. But Crash tells Penn to lean in, and Penn wins the race.

4. The Springfield team comes in second place in the Penn Relays. Penn, who runs the anchor, brings the team from last place to second.

5. Scooter climbs the stairs to see the photo of himself in his Navy uniform.

6. Crash spends his sneaker money on paints for his mother because he wants her to paint family portraits again.

7. Crash's mother cuts her work to part-time and takes an active interest in her family again. Crash's mother saves money by shopping at garage sales, shopping at thrift stores, and using coupons. His father doesn't change much, but Crash hopes that he'll make time for the family.

8. Crash becomes kinder, more loving toward his family. He and Penn become best friends. He helps his sister with her wildlife habitat and cares for Scooter. Jane Forbes invites Crash to a party at the end of the novel.

Page 43

Matching

1. c	6. g
2. j	7. i
3. d	8. f
4. b	9. e
5. h	10. a

True or False

1. True	4. False
2. False	5. True
3. True	

Short Answer

1. Crash's family is a contemporary two-parent working family. They spend little time together. They live in a nice home and are up to date on all the latest trends. Penn's family are vegetarian, peace-loving people. They live in a very modest house and don't have a TV. Penn's parents are very supportive and enjoy spending time together.

2. Penn, Abby and Jane value preservation of the environment and living lightly on the earth. They protest the development of land for a new mall and nurture turtles and other wildlife.

3. Crash may tackle his grandfather because he's feeling bad about a lot of things that aren't going well in his life at that time. He may also tackle him because he's upset at Scooter for not filming his game. Scooter almost makes a point for his team, so Crash tries to stop him. Crash was upset at realizing his grandfather was getting old.

4. The gift to Penn's great grandfather is Penn winning the race at the Penn Relays. It's an important gift because Penn and his great-grandfather were named after the Penn Relays. Crash tells Penn how to win the race-off so that he can participate in the Penn Relays.

Essay
Accept all reasonable answers pertaining to Crash's change in attitude toward Penn.

Page 44
Accept all reasonable and well-supported responses and explanations.

Page 45
Perform the conversations in class. Ask students to respond to conversations by asking the following: "Are the conversations true to the story?" and "Are the characters' words in keeping with their personalities?"